Published By Robert Corbin

@ Jim York

Dash Diet: Flavorsome Secrets to Boost Your

Wellness Today

All Right RESERVED

ISBN 978-87-94477-78-9

TABLE OF CONTENTS

Walnut Chia Overnight Oats 1

Kale Pineapple Smoothie 3

Melon And Raw Ham 5

Mixed Grilled Vegetables With Yogurt Sauce 7

Avocado Dip With Whole Grain Nachos 10

Greek Yogurt Parfait 13

Oatmeal With Berries 15

Vegetable Omelette 17

Grilled Chicken Or Fish With Roasted Vegetable 20

Grilled Balsamic Chicken With Roasted Asparagus And Mushrooms 22

Cauliflower And Broccoli 24

Greek Salad With Chicken 26

Sweet Potato And Chickpea Salad 28

Chickpea And Vegetable Stir-Fry With Brown Rice 29

Grilled Shrimp Skewers With Grilled Zucchini And Quinoa. 31

Smoothie Bowl With Frozen Berries, Greek Yogurt, And Granola. 33

Veggie Omelet 35

Greek Yogurt Parfait 37

Overnight Chia Pudding 38

Grilled Zucchini And Corn Salad With Fresh Herbs 40

Tangy Cabbage And Apple Slaw With Dijon Vinaigrette 42

Couscous Salad With Olives And Feta 44

White Bean Soup With Pasta 46

Peppery Shrimp In A Barbecue Sauce With Vegetables And Orzo 48

Ragu With Chicken And Mushrooms 51

Greek Yogurt Parfait 54

Vegetable Omelet 56

Overnight Chia Seed Pudding 59

Yogurt Parfait With Pumpkin 61

Veggie Omelet 63

Grilled Shrimp Skewers 66

Mixed Bean Salad With Celery And Parsley 69

Spinach And Ricotta Flans 71

Avocado Toast With Poached Egg 74

Grilled Garlic Herb Chicken With Roasted Brussels Sprouts And Carrots 77

Grilled Teriyaki Salmon With Roasted Green Beans And Red Cabbage 80

Egg Salad Lettuce Wraps 83

Baked Cod With Lemon And Herbs 84

Tuna Salad With Mixed Greens And Whole-Grain Crackers. 85

Baked Chicken With Roasted Brussels Sprouts And Sweet Potato Wedges. 87

Whole-Grain Pancakes With Fresh Fruit And Maple Syrup 89

Quinoa Breakfast Bowl 91

Vegetable Frittata 92

Oatmeal With Berries And Almonds 94

Roasted Cauliflower And Chickpea Salad With Tahini Dressing 96

Watermelon And Feta Salad With Mint And Balsamic Glaze 99

Grilled Portobello Mushroom And Quinoa Salad With Lemon Vinaigrette 100

Meal-Prep Chili-Lime Chicken Bowls 103

Chopped Cobb Salad 105

Banana Nut Pancakes 107

Smoothie Bowl 110

Egg And Spinach Breakfast Wrap 112

Mediterranean Breakfast Bowls 114

Mango Ginger Smoothie Bowl 116

Raspberry Overnight Muesli 118

Grilled Eggplant With Tomato Sauce And Oregano 119

Black Olive Paté With Croutons Of Whole Meal Bread 122

Smoked Salmon Mousse With Whole Meal Crackers .. 125

Pineapple Coconut Smoothie 128

Oat Bran With Berries 130

- Quinoa Breakfast Porridge 132
- Whole Grain Pasta Dishes With Tomatoes Sauce 134
- Whole Grain Penne With Roasted Tomatoes And Garlic Sauce 136
- Whole Wheat Fairdale With Tomato, Spinach, And Mushroom Sauce 138
- Tomato Basil Quiche 140
- Grilled Lemon Herb Salmon 141
- Grilled Vegetable Wrap With Hummus And Baby Carrots. 142
- Black Bean And Vegetable Chili With A Side Of Whole-Grain Cornbread. 144
- Greek Yogurt With Sliced Peaches And Chopped Almonds. 148

Walnut Chia Overnight Oats

Ingredients:

- ½ cup or 120ml Cashew Milk
- 14 Walnuts Halves or 30gm
- 3 to 4 or 20gm Berries of your choice
- Sweetener of your choice, preferably less
- 1 tbsp. or 15gm Chia Seeds
- 1 cup or 80gm Rolled Oats
- 1 tsp. Or 4.2gm Vanilla Extract

Directions:

1. First, combine rolled oats and chia seeds in a medium-sized bowl.
2. Next, pour in the milk and vanilla extract to it. Mix well.

3. Transfer the mixture to mason jars or bowls and refrigerate it overnight.
4. Top it with chopped walnuts and berries before serving.

Kale Pineapple Smoothie

Ingredients:

- ½ cup or 105gm Pineapple, cued

- 1/3 cup or 81gm Greek-Yogurt, plain & non-fat or Soy Yogurt

- 1 tsp. or 7gm Honey, optional

- ½ cup Ice, optional

- 1 cup or 30gm Kale

- 1 tbsp. or 15gm Chia Seeds

- ½ cup or 120ml Almond Milk, unsweetened

Directions:

1. Begin by pouring milk and yogurt into a high-speed blender and then stir in kale, pineapple, and chia seeds.

2. Blend for 1 to 2 minutes on high speed or until smooth and frothy. If adding ice, add now and blend again for another 1 minute.
3. Transfer to a serving glass and enjoy.

Melon And Raw Ham

Ingredients:

- 100-150g of thin slices of raw ham
- Fresh mint leaves (optional)
- 1 ripe melon (preferably cantaloupe or yellow melon)
- Ground black pepper.

Directions:

1. Cut the melon in half and remove the seeds in the center. Also remove the outer husk.
2. Cut the melon into slices or wedges of a suitable size for the appetizer.
3. Wrap each melon slice with a slice of raw ham. You can also fold or curl the ham for a more decorative presentation.

4. Arrange the melon and ham slices on a serving platter.
5. If you like, you can garnish with some fresh mint leaves for a touch of freshness and a more aesthetically pleasing dish.
6. Add a pinch of freshly ground black pepper over the melon and ham slices.
7. Serve melon and raw ham as a simple and delicious appetizer.
8. This classic combination of the sweetness of the melon and the saltiness of the cured ham is very popular. You can customize this recipe by adding diced fresh cheese or adding a splash of reduced balsamic vinegar for an extra kick of flavor. The melon and raw ham is an ideal appetizer for the summer or for any occasion in which you want a quick but tasty preparation.

Mixed Grilled Vegetables With Yogurt Sauce

Ingredients:

- 1 eggplant
- 1 red onion
- Extra virgin olive oil
- Salt and pepper.
- 1 red pepper
- 1 yellow pepper
- 1 curette

for the yogurt sauce:

- 1 clove of garlic, finely chopped
- 2 tablespoons of chopped fresh parsley
- Salt and pepper.

- 200g of Greek yogurt

- Juice of 1/2 lemon

Directions:

1. Preheat a grill or grill pan over medium-high heat.
2. Cut the peppers in half, remove the seeds and cut into strips. Cut the courgette, eggplant and onion into slices of uniform thickness.
3. Brush the vegetables with a drizzle of extra virgin olive oil and season with salt and pepper.
4. Place the vegetables on the grill or grill pan and cook until tender and slightly charred, turning occasionally.
5. Meanwhile, make the yogurt dip by mixing together the Greek yogurt, lemon juice, minced garlic, and fresh parsley. Season with salt and pepper according to your personal taste.

6. Transfer the grilled vegetables to a serving platter and serve with the yogurt dip as a topping.
7. You can also garnish with some chopped fresh parsley for an extra presentation.
8. Enjoy mixed grilled vegetables with yogurt sauce as a healthy and delicious appetizer.
9. You can customize this recipe by adding other vegetables such as mushrooms, asparagus or cherry tomatoes. Grilled vegetables are a versatile and tasty choice for an appetizer or side dish. The yogurt sauce adds a nice crispness and creaminess.

Avocado Dip With Whole Grain Nachos

Ingredients:

- 1/4 red onion, finely chopped
- 2 tablespoons chopped fresh coriander
- Salt and pepper
- 2 ripe avocados
- Juice of 1 lemon
- 1 clove of garlic, finely chopped
- Whole grain nachos to serve.

Directions:

1. Cut the avocados in half, remove the stone and scoop out the pulp. Put the avocado pulp in a bowl.

2. Squeeze lemon juice over the avocado pulp to prevent oxidation and add a fresh flavor.
3. Mash the avocados with a fork or blend them briefly until you get a creamy texture.
4. Add the finely chopped garlic, red onion, and cilantro to the bowl with the avocados.
5. Mix the ingredients until you get a homogeneous mixture. You can leave the sauce slightly more rustic or keep stirring to make it smoother.
6. Season with salt and pepper, according to your personal taste.
7. Serve avocado dip with whole-grain nachos as a tasty and healthy appetizer.
8. You can customize this recipe by adding ingredients like crushed fresh chili for a kick of heat or diced tomatoes for a fresher salsa.
9. Be sure to use ripe avocados for a creamy texture and rich flavor.

10. This avocado dip is perfect as an accompaniment to whole-grain nachos or as a topping for tacos and burritos.

Greek Yogurt Parfait

Ingredients:

- 2 tablespoons honey or maple syrup
- 1/4 cup granola
- 1 tablespoon chopped nuts (almonds, walnuts, or pistachios)
- 1 cup Greek yogurt
- 1/2 cup mixed berries (strawberries, blueberries, raspberries)
- Fresh mint leaves for garnish (optional)

Directions:

1. In a glass or bowl, start by layering half of the Greek yogurt. Add a portion of the mixed berries on top of the yogurt layer.

2. Drizzle a tablespoon of honey or maple syrup over the berries. Sprinkle a portion of granola and chopped nuts on top of the berries.
3. Repeat the layering process with the remaining yogurt, berries, honey, granola, and nuts. Garnish with fresh mint leaves if desired. Serve chilled.

Oatmeal With Berries

Ingredients:

- 1/2 cup mixed berries (strawberries, blueberries, raspberries)
- 1 tablespoon honey or maple syrup
- 1 tablespoon chia seeds (optional)
- 1 tablespoon chopped nuts (almonds, walnuts, or pecans)
- 1/2 cup rolled oats
- 1 cup water or milk (dairy or plant-based)
- A pinch of cinnamon (optional)

Directions:

1. In a saucepan, bring the water or milk to a boil. Add the rolled oats and reduce the heat to a simmer.
2. Cook for around 5-7 minutes, stirring occasionally, until the oats reach the desired texture.
3. Once cooked, move the oatmeal to a bowl. Top it with a mix of berries, drizzle with honey or maple syrup, add chia seeds (if desired), chopped nuts, and a pinch of cinnamon for extra flavor. Serve warm.

Vegetable Omelette

Ingredients:

- 1/4 cup chopped spinach or kale
- 1 tablespoon chopped onion
- 1 tablespoon chopped fresh herbs (parsley or cilantro)
- 1 tablespoon olive oil
- Salt and pepper to taste
- 2 eggs
- 1/4 cup chopped bell peppers (red, green, or yellow)
- 1/4 cup diced tomatoes
- 1/4 cup grated low-fat cheese (optional)

Directions:

1. In a bowl, whisk the eggs until they are thoroughly mixed.
2. Heat some olive oil in a non-stick skillet over medium heat. Add the chopped bell peppers, onions, and sauté until they are slightly softened.
3. Then, add the diced tomatoes and chopped spinach or kale, cooking until the vegetables are tender but still have a bit of crunch.
4. Pour the beaten eggs evenly over the vegetables in the skillet. Let the eggs set around the edges.
5. Use a spatula to gently lift the edges, tilting the skillet to let the uncooked eggs flow underneath.
6. Once the eggs are mostly cooked, sprinkle with fresh herbs and grated cheese (if desired).
7. Fold the omelets in half and cook for another minute until the cheese melts.

8. Slide the omelets onto a plate, season with salt and pepper to taste, and serve hot.

Grilled Chicken Or Fish With Roasted Vegetable

Ingredients:

- 1 tsp dried oregano
- Salt and pepper to taste
- 2 bell peppers, sliced
- 1 zucchini, sliced
- Olive oil
- 4 boneless, skinless chicken breasts
- 2 cloves of garlic, minced
- Juice of 1 lemon
- Fresh parsley for garnish

Directions:

1. In a small bowl, mix the minced garlic, lemon juice, oregano, salt, and pepper.
2. Place the chicken breasts in a shallow dish and drizzle with the marinade. marinate the chicken for 30 minutes.
3. Preheat your grill to medium heat.
4. In a separate bowl, toss the sliced bell peppers and zucchini with a drizzle of olive oil and a sprinkle of salt.
5. Place the bell peppers and zucchini on a grill basket and place on the grill. Grill for 8-10 minutes, or until slightly charred and tender.
6. Grill the chicken for 6-7 minutes on each side, or until the internal temperature reaches 165°F.
7. Serve the grilled lemon garlic chicken with the roasted bell peppers and zucchini on the side. Garnish with fresh parsley if desired.

Grilled Balsamic Chicken With Roasted Asparagus And Mushrooms

Ingredients:

- 1 tsp dried thyme
- Salt and pepper to taste
- 1 bunch asparagus, cut woody ends
- 1 cup sliced mushrooms
- 4 boneless, skinless chicken breasts
- 1/4 cup balsamic vinegar
- 2 tbsp olive oil
- 2 cloves of garlic, minced
- Fresh thyme for garnish

Directions:

1. In a small bowl, whisk together the balsamic vinegar, olive oil, minced garlic, dried thyme, salt, and pepper.
2. Place the chicken breasts in a shallow dish and drizzle with the marinade. marinade the chicken for 30 minutes.
3. Preheat your grill to medium heat.
4. Place the marinated chicken on the grill and grill for 6-7 minutes on each side, or until the internal temperature reaches 165°F.
5. In a separate bowl, toss the asparagus and mushrooms with a drizzle of olive oil and a sprinkle of salt and pepper.
6. Place the asparagus and mushrooms on a grill basket and place on the grill. Grill for 8-10 minutes, or until the asparagus is tender and the mushrooms are slightly charred.
7. Serve the grilled balsamic chicken with roasted asparagus and mushrooms. Garnish with fresh thyme if desired.

Cauliflower And Broccoli

Ingredients:

- 1 tsp garlic powder
- Salt and pepper to taste
- 1 cauliflower head, cut into florets.
- 1 broccoli head, cut into florets
- Olive oil
- 4 white fish fillets (tilapia, cod, halibut)
- 2 tbsp Cajun seasoning
- 2 tbsp olive oil
- Lemon wedges for serving

Directions:

1. In a small bowl, mix the Cajun seasoning, olive oil, garlic powder, salt, and pepper.
2. Rub the seasoning mixture on both sides of the fish fillets.
3. Preheat your grill to medium heat.
4. Place the fish fillets on the grill and grill for 4-5 minutes on each side, or until the fish is flaky and cooked through.
5. In a separate bowl, toss the cauliflower and broccoli with a drizzle of olive oil and a sprinkle of salt and pepper.
6. Place the cauliflower and broccoli on a grill basket and place on the grill. Grill for 10-12 minutes, or until the vegetables are tender and slightly charred.
7. Serve the grilled Cajun fish with the roasted cauliflower and broccoli. Squeeze a lemon wedge over the fish before serving.

Greek Salad With Chicken

Ingredients:

- Cherry tomatoes
- Cucumber, diced
- Kalamata olives
- Feta cheese
- Grilled chicken breast, sliced
- Mixed greens
- Olive oil and balsamic vinegar dressing

Directions:

1. Arrange mixed greens on a plate.
2. Top with sliced grilled chicken, tomatoes, cucumber, olives, and feta.

3. Drizzle with olive oil and balsamic vinegar dressing.

Sweet Potato And Chickpea Salad

Ingredients:

- Chickpeas, drained and rinsed
- Red onion, finely chopped
- Spinach leaves
- Sweet potatoes, diced
- Lemon vinaigrette dressing

Directions:

1. Roast sweet potatoes until tender.
2. Mix roasted sweet potatoes, chickpeas, red onion, and spinach.
3. Drizzle with lemon vinaigrette.

Chickpea And Vegetable Stir-Fry With Brown Rice

Ingredients:

- 1 red bell pepper, sliced
- 1 zucchini, sliced
- 1 cup sliced mushrooms
- 1 can chickpeas, drained and rinsed
- 2 tablespoons soy sauce
- 1 tablespoon cornstarch
- 1 teaspoon honey
- 1 cup cooked brown rice
- 1 tablespoon vegetable oil
- 1 small onion, diced

- 2 cloves garlic, minced

- 1/4 teaspoon red pepper flakes (optional)

Directions:

1. Heat the vegetable oil in a large skillet or wok over medium-high heat.
2. Add the onion and garlic and sauté for 2-3 minutes, or until the onion is translucent.
3. Add the red bell pepper, zucchini, and mushrooms and stir-fry for 5-7 minutes, or until the vegetables are tender.
4. Add the chickpeas and stir to combine.
5. In a small bowl, whisk together the soy sauce, cornstarch, honey, and red pepper flakes (if using).
6. Pour the sauce into the skillet and stir until the vegetables and chickpeas are coated and the sauce has thickened.
7. Serve the stir-fry over a bed of cooked brown rice.

Grilled Shrimp Skewers With Grilled Zucchini And Quinoa.

Ingredients:

- 2 tablespoons olive oil
- 2 cloves garlic, minced
- 1/2 teaspoon salt
- 1/4 teaspoon black pepper
- 1 pound large shrimp, peeled and deveined
- 2 medium zucchinis, sliced into rounds
- 1 cup quinoa, rinsed and drained
- 2 cups water
- Wooden skewers

Directions:

1. Preheat grill to medium-high heat.
2. In a saucepan, bring the quinoa and water to a boil. Reduce heat to low and simmer for 15-20 minutes, until the quinoa is cooked and the water is absorbed.
3. In a small bowl, mix together the olive oil, garlic, salt, and black pepper.
4. Thread the shrimp onto the wooden skewers and brush with the olive oil mixture.
5. Brush the zucchini rounds with the olive oil mixture.
6. Place the shrimp skewers and zucchini rounds on the grill and cook for 3-4 minutes per side, or until the shrimp are pink and cooked through and the zucchini is tender and slightly charred.
7. Serve the shrimp and zucchini skewers over the quinoa.

Smoothie Bowl With Frozen Berries, Greek Yogurt, And Granola.

Ingredients:

- 1/2 cup unsweetened almond milk (or milk of your choice)
- 1 tablespoon honey (optional)
- 1/2 cup granola
- 1 cup frozen mixed berries (such as strawberries, blueberries, and raspberries)
- 1/2 cup plain Greek yogurt
- Toppings of your choice (such as fresh fruit, nuts, or seeds)

Directions:

1. In a blender, combine the frozen berries, Greek yogurt, almond milk, and honey (if using). Blend until smooth.
2. Pour the smoothie mixture into a bowl.
3. Top the smoothie bowl with granola and any additional toppings of your choice.
4. Serve and enjoy!

Veggie Omelet

Ingredients:

- 1/4 cup chopped onions
- 1/4 cup chopped tomatoes
- 1/4 cup chopped spinach
- Salt and pepper to taste
- 2 large eggs
- a quarter cup of colored bell peppers, chopped
- Cooking spray

Directions:

1. In a bowl, whisk the eggs with salt and pepper.

2. Heat a non-stick skillet over medium heat and coat it with cooking spray.
3. Add the bell peppers, onions, and tomatoes to the skillet. Sauté for 2 to 3 minutes or until softened somewhat.
4. Add the spinach and cook for another minute until wilted.
5. Pour the whisked eggs into the skillet, spreading them evenly.
6. Cook for 2-3 minutes until the eggs are set, then carefully flip the omelet and cook for another minute.
7. Transfer to a plate, fold in half, and serve.

Greek Yogurt Parfait

Ingredients:

- 1 tablespoon honey
- 2 tablespoons granola
- 1 cup plain Greek yogurt
- 1/4 cup mixed berries (blueberries, strawberries, raspberries)

Directions:
1. In a glass or bowl, layer half of the Greek yogurt.
2. Add half of the mixed berries on top of the yogurt.
3. Drizzle half of the honey over the berries.
4. Sprinkle 1 tablespoon of granola.
5. Layer the remaining ingredients once more.
6. Serve chilled.

Overnight Chia Pudding

Ingredients:

- 1 cup unsweetened almond milk
- 1/4 teaspoon vanilla extract
- 1 tablespoon honey or maple syrup
- 2 tablespoons chia seeds
- Sliced fruits and nuts for topping

Directions:

1. In a jar or container, combine chia seeds, almond milk, vanilla extract, and sweetener.
2. Stir well to combine and make sure the chia seeds are fully immersed in the liquid.
3. Cover the jar and refrigerate overnight or for at least 4 hours.
4. Stir the mixture before serving to ensure a pudding-like consistency.

5. Top with sliced fruits and nuts of your choice.

Grilled Zucchini And Corn Salad With Fresh Herbs

Ingredients:

- Use 2 tablespoon of olive oil
- Use 1 tablespoon of balsamic vinegar
- Use 1 tablespoon of chopped fresh basil
- Use 1 tablespoon of chopped fresh parsley
- 2 medium zucchinis, sliced lengthwise
- 2 ears of corn, husked
- Salt and pepper to taste

Directions:

1. Preheat a grill or grill pan over medium-high heat.
2. Brush the zucchini slices and corn with olive oil, then season with salt and pepper.

3. Grill the zucchini slices for 2-3 minutes per side, or until grill marks appear and the zucchini is tender. Set aside.
4. Grill the corn for 8-10 minutes, turning occasionally, until the kernels are slightly charred. Let it cool, then cut the kernels off the cob.
5. In a large bowl, mix the grilled zucchini slices, grilled corn kernels, balsamic vinegar, chopped basil, and chopped parsley. Toss gently to mix.
6. Season with additional salt and pepper if needed.
7. Serve the grilled zucchini and corn salad with fresh herbs immediately.

Tangy Cabbage And Apple Slaw With Dijon Vinaigrette

Ingredients:

To prepare Slaw:

- 1/4 cup chopped red onion
- 1/4 cup chopped fresh parsley
- 1/4 cup chopped fresh dill
- 4 cups shredded green cabbage
- 2 apples, cored and thinly sliced

To prepare Dijon Vinaigrette:

- Use 2 tablespoon of apple cider vinegar
- Use 1 tablespoon of Dijon mustard
- 1 teaspoon honey or maple syrup

- 3 tablespoons extra-virgin olive oil
- Salt and pepper to taste

Directions:

1. In a large bowl, mix the shredded green cabbage, thinly sliced apples, chopped red onion, chopped fresh parsley, and chopped fresh dill.
2. In a separate bowl, whisk together the extra-virgin olive oil, apple cider vinegar, Dijon mustard, honey or maple syrup, salt, and pepper to make the Dijon vinaigrette.
3. Drizzle the vinaigrette over the slaw and toss gently to ensure all ingredients are coated.
4. Serve the tangy cabbage and apple slaw immediately.

Couscous Salad With Olives And Feta

Ingredients:

- 1 teaspoon dried oregano
- Use 1 cup of cherry tomatoes, halved
- 1/2 cup pitted Kalamata olives, sliced
- 1/2 cup crumbled feta cheese
- 1/4 cup chopped fresh parsley
- Use 1 cup of couscous
- 1 1/4 cups water or vegetable broth
- 1/4 cup extra-virgin olive oil
- Use 2 tablespoon of red wine vinegar
- Salt and pepper to taste

Directions:

1. In a saucepan, bring the water or vegetable broth to a boil. Stir in the couscous, cover the saucepan, and remove it from the heat. Let it sit for 5 minutes, then fluff with a fork.
2. In a large bowl, whisk together the extra-virgin olive oil, red wine vinegar, and dried oregano to make the dressing.
3. Add the cooked couscous, cherry tomatoes, sliced Kalamata olives, crumbled feta cheese, and chopped fresh parsley to the bowl with the dressing.
4. Toss all the ingredients gently to ensure they are well mix.
5. Season with salt and pepper according to your taste preferences.
6. Serve the Mediterranean couscous salad with olives and feta immediately.

White Bean Soup With Pasta

Ingredients:

- 1 teaspoon of salt

- 1/4 teaspoon of crushed red pepper

- 1/4 teaspoon of ground pepper

- 1 (28-ounce) can of no-salt-added diced tomatoes • 2 cups of low-sodium no-chicken broth or chicken broth

- 1 tablespoon of extra-virgin olive oil

- 1 1/2 cups of frozen mirepoix (diced onion, celery, and carrot)

- 2 cloves of minced garlic

- 1 teaspoon of Italian seasoning

Directions:

1. Bring a big pot of water to a boil.
2. Heat oil over medium-high heat in a large pot. Add the mirepoix and cook, stirring, for about 3 minutes, until it softens.
3. Add the garlic, Italian seasoning, salt, crushed red pepper, and ground pepper and stir while cooking for about a minute, or until the smell is nice. Bring to a boil the tomatoes and their juices, the broth, and the beans.
4. Turn down the heat to keep a lively simmer. Cover and cook, stirring every so often, for about 10 minutes, or until the tomatoes start to break down.
5. While the water boils, cook the pasta for 1 minute less than what the package says. Drain.
6. Add spinach to the soup and mix it in. Mix the pasta in right before you serve it. Serve with Parmesan cheese on top.

Peppery Shrimp In A Barbecue Sauce With Vegetables And Orzo

Ingredients:

- 1 cup whole-grain orzo
- 3 scallions
- 2 tablespoons olive oil, divided
- 2 cups coarsely chopped zucchini
- 1 cup coarsely chopped bell pepper
- Lemon wedges to put on the table
- 1 pound peeled and deveined jumbo shrimp, thawed if frozen (see Tip)
- 1 teaspoon paprika
- 1/2 teaspoon garlic powder

- 1/2 teaspoon crushed dried oregano
- 1/4 teaspoon ground pepper
- 1/8 teaspoon cayenne pepper

Directions:

1. Put the shrimp in a medium-sized bowl. In a small bowl, mix together the paprika, garlic powder, oregano, pepper, and cayenne. Sprinkle the spice mix over the shrimp, toss to coat, and set aside.
2. Bring a lot of water to a boil in a large pot. Cook orzo according to the Directions: on the package, then drain. Put it back in the hot pot, cover it, and keep it warm.
3. Slice the scallions, making sure to separate the white and green parts. In a medium-sized pan, heat 1 tablespoon of oil over medium-high heat.
4. Add the white parts of the scallions, zucchini, bell pepper, and celery.

5. Cook, stirring every so often, for about 5 minutes, or until the vegetables are crisp-tender.
6. Add the tomatoes and cook for another 2 to 3 minutes, until they are soft. Mix the vegetables in with the orzo in the pot. Add salt and mix together.
7. Heat the last tablespoon of oil in the same pan over medium heat. Add the shrimp and cook for 4 to 6 minutes, turning them once, until they are opaque.
8. Put barbecue sauce on top. About a minute of cooking and stirring is all it takes to coat the shrimp.
9. Mix the vegetables and serve them with the shrimp. If you want, you can serve it with wedges of lemon on top.

Ragu With Chicken And Mushrooms

Ingredients:

- 1 34 pounds boneless, skinless chicken thighs, trimmed and cut into 1-inch pieces
- 2 cloves grated garlic
- 14 cup tomato paste
- 12 cup dry red wine
- 12 teaspoon salt
- 14 teaspoon crushed red pepper
- 1 tablespoon chopped fresh rosemary
- 1 28-ounce can of whole, peeled, no-salt-added San Marzano tomatoes
- 14 cup extra-virgin olive oil

- 1 medium onion, chopped

- 2 medium carrots, chopped

- 8 ounces cremini mushrooms, quartered

- 1 pound whole-wheat ling

Directions:

1. Bring a big pot of water to a boil.
2. Pour the tomato juice and tomatoes into a medium bowl. Break up the tomatoes into chunks with your hands.
3. Heat oil in an electric pressure cooker on Sauté mode. Add the onion, carrots, and mushrooms.
4. Cook, stirring, for about 5 minutes, or until the mushrooms have given off their liquid. Mix in the chicken, garlic, and tomato paste.
5. Cook, stirring every now and then, for about 4 minutes, or until the chicken is coated and the mixture at the bottom of the pan is starting to

brown. Add the wine, salt, red pepper flakes, and tomatoes.
6. Cook, scraping up the browned bits, for about 2 minutes, or until the liquid starts to boil. Put out the fire.
7. Close the lid and lock it. For 10 minutes, cook at high pressure. Let go of the pressure by hand. Add rosemary and mix.
8. Cook the pasta according to the Directions: on the package. Drain the pasta, then serve it with the sauce, cheese, and parsley on top.

Greek Yogurt Parfait

Ingredients:

- Fresh Berries (e.g., strawberries, blueberries, raspberries): 1/2 cup

- Granola (unsweetened or low-sugar): 1/4 cup

- Honey or Maple Syrup (optional): 1 tablespoon

- Greek Yogurt (unsweetened): 1 cup

- Nuts or Seeds (e.g., almonds, chia seeds): 1 tablespoon (optional)

Directions:

1. Scoop 1 cup of unsweetened Greek yogurt into a bowl.
2. Rinse and slice fresh berries of your choice.
3. In a glass or bowl, layer Greek yogurt with a portion of the sliced berries.

4. Sprinkle 1/4 cup of unsweetened or low-sugar granola on top of the yogurt and berries.
5. If desired, add a touch of sweetness with 1 tablespoon of honey or maple syrup.
6. For added crunch and nutrition, sprinkle 1 tablespoon of nuts or seeds on top.
7. Repeat the layering process until you fill the glass or bowl, ending with a final layer of berries and a drizzle of honey if desired.
8. If you're meal prepping, cover and refrigerate for later. Otherwise, enjoy your Greek Yogurt Parfait immediately.

Vegetable Omelet

Ingredients:

- 1/4 cup red onion (finely chopped)
- 1/4 cup spinach leaves (chopped)
- 1/4 cup mushrooms (sliced)
- Salt and pepper to taste
- 1 tablespoon olive oil or cooking spray for the pan
- 2 large eggs
- 1/4 cup bell peppers (diced, assorted colors)
- 1/4 cup tomatoes (diced)
- Optional: 1/4 cup shredded cheese (such as feta or cheddar)

Directions:

1. Dice the bell peppers and tomatoes, chop the spinach leaves, finely chop the red onion, and slice the mushrooms.
2. In a bowl, whisk the eggs until well combined. Add a pinch of salt and pepper to taste.
3. Heat olive oil or use cooking spray in a non-stick skillet over medium heat.
4. Sauté the red onion until translucent, then add the bell peppers, tomatoes, mushrooms, and spinach. Cook until vegetables are tender.
5. Pour the whisked eggs over the sautéed vegetables evenly. Allow the eggs to set around the edges.
6. If using cheese, sprinkle it over one half of the omelet.
7. Once the eggs are almost set, carefully fold the omelet in half, covering the cheese if added.
8. Cook for an additional minute until the eggs are fully cooked but still moist.

9. Slide the omelet onto a plate, and season with additional salt and pepper if needed.

Overnight Chia Seed Pudding

Ingredients:

- 1-2 tablespoons maple syrup or honey (adjust to taste)
- 1/2 teaspoon vanilla extract
- Fresh fruits (e.g., berries, sliced banana) for topping
- 1/4 cup chia seeds
- 1 cup unsweetened almond milk (or any milk of your choice)
- Nuts or seeds (e.g., sliced almonds, chia seeds) for garnish

Directions:

1. In a bowl or jar, combine chia seeds, almond milk, maple syrup (or honey), and vanilla extract.
2. Stir well to ensure the chia seeds are evenly distributed in the liquid.
3. Cover the bowl or jar and refrigerate overnight or for at least 4 hours.
4. You can give it a gentle stir after the first 30 minutes to prevent clumping.
5. Before serving, give the pudding a good stir as it may thicken unevenly.
6. Top with fresh fruits and nuts or seeds of your choice.

Yogurt Parfait With Pumpkin

Ingredients:

- 1 tbsp. or 15gm Pumpkin Puree

- 1 tsp. or 4.2gm Vanilla Extract

- ½ tbsp. or 3.5gm Flax Seeds

- Dash of Cinnamon, ground

- 1 cup or 254gm plain, low-fat Greek Yogurt or Soy Yogurt

- 1 tbsp. or 7.45gm Pumpkin Seeds

- Liquid Sweetener of your choice, optional

Directions:

1. Start by filling the mason jar with yogurt. Spoon in the vanilla essence and mix well.

2. Next, add the remaining ingredients to the mason jar.
3. Close the lid and refrigerate until it needs to be served. Stir only before eating so that the topping doesn't get soggy. If you prefer it soggy, stir before storing.

Veggie Omelet

Ingredients:

- 1 tbsp. Onion or 3.25gm, diced
- 1 tbsp. or 15.3gm Milk, low-fat
- Black Pepper, as needed
- ¼ cup Corn or 68gm, quartered
- 2 Eggs or 80gm
- ½ of 1 Broccoli or 100gm, small & diced
- Kosher Salt, as needed
- 2 tbsp. or 28gm Cheddar Cheese, sharp & low-fat

Directions:

1. Begin by heating a small non-stick skillet over medium heat. Grease it with olive oil spray.

Tip: A 6-inch or 8-inch pan would be ideal for a 2-egg omelet.

2. Whisk the egg for a minute or until it is pale yellow in color. Tip: Do not overbeat.
3. After that, beat the eggs, milk, salt, and pepper in another bowl with 1 teaspoon of water until mixed well. Tip: When we whisk well, we can add more air to the eggs. And more air means a fluffier omelet.
4. Next, pour the eggs into the skillet and cook for a minute or until the egg is slightly set at the center. Do not stir. Cook for another 2 to 3 minutes or until they bubble up and pull away from the sides of the pan.
5. Then, stir in 1/2 of the cheese on one side of the omelet, and top with veggies. Add the remaining cheese. Tip: If desired, you can sauté the veggies for a few minutes so that they are lightly softened and more flavorful.

But then, if you prefer crunchiness, you can add the veggies as it is.
6. Fold the bare side over the side with the fillings and cook for 2 minutes.
7. Turn and cook for 2 minutes before transferring to the plate.
8. Serve hot and enjoy. Garnish it with mint leaves and parsley for more flavor.

Grilled Shrimp Skewers

Ingredients:

- 2 cloves of garlic, finely chopped
- Salt and pepper
- 1 red bell pepper, diced
- 1 red onion, diced
- 16-20 large shrimp, peeled and gutted
- Juice of 1 lemon
- 2 tablespoons of extra virgin olive oil
- Wooden or metal skewers, previously soaked in water (if you use wooden skewers).

Directions:

1. Start by preparing a marinade for the shrimp. In a bowl, mix together the lemon juice, extra virgin olive oil, minced garlic, salt, and pepper.
2. Add the shrimp to the marinade and mix well to make sure they are completely coated. Marinate the shrimp in the refrigerator for at least 30 minutes to allow the flavors to develop.
3. Meanwhile, prepare the bell pepper and onion by cutting them into cubes of the same size.
4. Prepare the kebabs by alternating the marinated shrimp, bell pepper and onion on the sticks.
5. Preheat the grill over medium-high heat.
6. Place the skewers on the grill and cook them for about 2 to 3 minutes per side, until the shrimp are pink and cooked through.

7. While cooking, you can brush the skewers with the remaining marinade to add extra flavor.
8. Once cooked, transfer the grilled shrimp skewers to a serving platter.
9. Serve the grilled shrimp skewers as a delicious and light appetizer.
10. You can customize this recipe by adding spices like sweet paprika, red pepper, or thyme to the marinade for an extra kick of flavor.
11. You can also add other veggies like zucchini or cherry tomatoes on the skewers for variety.
12. Grilled shrimp skewers are perfect for a summer barbecue or as an appetizer on any occasion.

Mixed Bean Salad With Celery And Parsley

Ingredients:

- Juice of 1 lemon

- 3 tablespoons of extra virgin olive oil

- Salt and pepper.

- 400 g of mixed beans (cannellini, borlotti, black, etc.), drained and rinsed

- 2 stalks of celery, cut into thin slices

- 1/2 red onion, thinly sliced

- 1 bunch of fresh parsley, chopped

Directions:

1. In a large bowl, combine the blended beans, sliced celery, red onion, and chopped parsley.

2. In a small bowl, make a simple vinaigrette by mixing together the lemon juice, olive oil, salt, and pepper.
3. Pour the vinaigrette over the bean and vegetable mixture and mix well to make sure everything is well seasoned.
4. Let the mixed bean salad sit in the refrigerator for at least 30 minutes to allow the flavors to meld.
5. Before serving, taste and adjust salt and pepper according to your personal taste.
6. Serve the mixed bean salad with celery and parsley as a light and healthy appetizer.
7. You can customize this recipe by adding other ingredients like halved cherry tomatoes, sliced black olives, or diced peppers to vary the flavors and textures of the salad.
8. This mixed bean salad is high in fiber and protein and is perfect for a light meal or as a side dish.

Spinach And Ricotta Flans

Ingredients:

- 2 eggs
- 30 g of grated cheese (such as parmesan or pecorino)
- 1 clove of garlic, finely chopped
- Salt and pepper
- 200 g of fresh spinach
- 200 g of cottage cheese
- Butter or olive oil to grease the ramekins.

Directions:

1. Preheat the oven to 180°C and prepare flan molds, greasing them with butter or olive oil.

2. In a pan, cook the spinach in a little olive oil until wilted. Add the minced garlic and cook for another 1-2 minutes.
3. Drain the spinach to remove excess water and transfer to a bowl.
4. Add the ricotta, eggs, grated cheese, salt, and pepper to the bowl with the spinach.
5. Mix all the ingredients together until you get a homogeneous mixture.
6. Pour the mixture into the prepared flan moulds, filling them up to 3/4 full.
7. Level the surface of the flans with the back of a spoon.
8. Place the ramekins on a baking sheet and bake in the preheated oven for about 20-25 minutes or until the ramekins are golden brown and firm to the touch.
9. Remove the flans from the oven and let them cool slightly before turning them out.

10. Unmold the spinach and ricotta flans onto serving plates.
11. Serve the flans as a hot appetizer or as a light side dish.
12. You can customize this recipe by adding ingredients like grated nutmeg or crushed red pepper flakes for an extra kick of flavor.
13. Spinach and ricotta flans are a tasty and healthy option, perfect for a light meal or as an appetizer.

Avocado Toast With Poached Egg

Ingredients:

- Salt and pepper to taste
- Red pepper flakes (optional)
- Fresh herbs (parsley or cilantro) for garnish (optional)
- 2 slices whole grain bread
- 1 ripe avocado
- 2 eggs
- Lemon wedges for serving (optional)

Directions:

1. Start by toasting the whole grain bread slices until they are a golden brown.

2. While that's happening, cut the avocado in half, remove the pit, and scoop out the flesh into a bowl.
3. Mash it up with a fork until it's the consistency you want, then season it with salt, pepper, and a pinch of red pepper flakes if you like.
4. Next, poach the eggs. Bring a pot of water to a gentle simmer, then crack one egg into a small bowl.
5. a whirlpool in the simmering water and carefully slide the egg into the center.
6. Cook for about 3-4 minutes until the whites are set but the yolk is still runny.
7. Take the poached egg out with a slotted spoon and repeat the process with the second egg.
8. Spread the mashed avocado onto the toasted bread slices, then place a poached egg on top of each one.

9. Sprinkle some salt, pepper, and extra red pepper flakes if you want.
10. Garnish with fresh herbs and serve with lemon wedges for extra flavor if you like.

Grilled Garlic Herb Chicken With Roasted Brussels Sprouts And Carrots

Ingredients:

- 2 tbsp chopped fresh rosemary
- 2 tbsp chopped fresh parsley
- Salt and pepper to taste
- 1 lb Brussels sprouts, halved
- 4 carrots, peeled and cut into sticks
- 4 boneless, skinless chicken breasts
- 3 cloves of garlic, minced
- 2 tbsp chopped fresh thyme
- Olive oil

Directions:

1. In a small bowl, mix the minced garlic, thyme, rosemary, parsley, salt, and pepper.
2. Place the chicken breasts in a shallow dish and rub the herb mixture on both sides of the chicken. marinate for 30 minutes.
3. Preheat your grill to medium heat.
4. Place the chicken on the grill and grill for 6-7 minutes on each side, or until the internal temperature reaches 165°F.
5. In a separate bowl, toss the Brussels sprouts and carrots with a drizzle of olive oil and a sprinkle of salt and pepper.
6. Place the vegetables on a grill basket and place on the grill.
7. Grill for 12-15 minutes, stirring occasionally, until the vegetables are tender and slightly charred.

8. Serve the grilled garlic herb chicken with the roasted Brussels sprouts and carrots on the side.

Grilled Teriyaki Salmon With Roasted Green Beans And Red Cabbage

Ingredients:

- 1 tsp grated ginger
- Salt and pepper to taste
- 1 lb green beans, trimmed
- 1 small head of red cabbage, chopped
- Olive oil
- 4 salmon fillets
- 1/4 cup teriyaki sauce
- 1 tbsp honey
- 1 tbsp soy sauce
- Sesame seeds for garnish

Directions:

1. In a small bowl, mix the teriyaki sauce, honey, soy sauce, grated ginger, salt, and pepper.
2. Pour the marinade over the salmon fillets and set aside.
3. Make sure the salmon is fully coated and let it marinate for at least 30 minutes.
4. Preheat your grill to medium heat.
5. Place the marinated salmon on the grill and grill for 4-5 minutes on each side, or until the salmon is cooked through.
6. In a separate bowl, toss the green beans and red cabbage with a drizzle of olive oil and a sprinkle of salt and pepper.
7. Place the vegetables on a grill basket and place them on the grill. Grill for 10-12 minutes, or until the vegetables are tender and slightly charred.
8. Serve the grilled teriyaki salmon with the roasted green beans and red cabbage.

Sprinkle sesame seeds over the salmon and vegetables before serving.

Egg Salad Lettuce Wraps

Ingredients:

- Hard-boiled eggs, chopped
- Greek yogurt
- Dijon mustard
- Celery, finely chopped
- Lettuce leaves

Directions:

1. Mix chopped eggs, Greek yogurt, Dijon mustard, and celery.
2. Spoon egg salad onto lettuce leaves.
3. Roll lettuce leaves to form wraps.

Baked Cod With Lemon And Herbs

Ingredients:

- Cod fillet
- Lemon slices
- Fresh herbs (such as dill or parsley)
- Olive oil

Directions:

1. Preheat oven to 400°F (200°C).
2. Place cod on a baking sheet, top with lemon slices and herbs.
3. Drizzle with olive oil and bake until fish flakes easily.

Tuna Salad With Mixed Greens And Whole-Grain Crackers.

Ingredients:

- 1/4 cup mayonnaise
- 1 tablespoon Dijon mustard
- 1 tablespoon lemon juice
- Salt and pepper, to taste
- Mixed greens
- 2 cans of tuna, drained
- 1/2 cup chopped celery
- 1/2 cup chopped red onion
- 1/4 cup chopped fresh parsley
- Whole-grain crackers

Directions:

1. In a large bowl, combine the tuna, celery, red onion, and parsley.
2. In a separate small bowl, whisk together the mayonnaise, Dijon mustard, lemon juice, salt, and pepper.
3. Pour the dressing over the tuna mixture and stir to combine.
4. Serve the tuna salad over a bed of mixed greens and with whole-grain crackers on the side.

Baked Chicken With Roasted Brussels Sprouts And Sweet Potato Wedges.

Ingredients:

- 2 sweet potatoes, cut into wedges
- 2 tablespoons olive oil
- 1 teaspoon garlic powder
- 1 teaspoon dried thyme
- 4 boneless, skinless chicken breasts
- 1 pound Brussels sprouts, trimmed and halved
- Salt and pepper to taste

Directions:

1. Preheat your oven to 400°F (200°C).

2. Season the chicken breasts with garlic powder, thyme, salt, and pepper. Place them in a baking dish.
3. In a separate bowl, toss the Brussels sprouts and sweet potato wedges with olive oil, salt, and pepper. Arrange them around the chicken in the baking dish.
4. Bake for 25-30 minutes, or until the chicken is cooked through and the vegetables are tender and crispy.
5. Serve and enjoy!

Whole-Grain Pancakes With Fresh Fruit And Maple Syrup.

Ingredients:

- 2 large sweet potatoes, cut into wedges
- 3 tbsp. olive oil
- 1 tsp. dried thyme
- 1 tsp. garlic powder
- 4 bone-in, skin-on chicken thighs
- 1 lb. Brussels sprouts, trimmed and halved
- Salt and pepper, to taste

Directions:

1. Preheat the oven to 425°F (218°C).

2. In a large bowl, toss Brussels sprouts and sweet potato wedges with 2 tbsp. olive oil, dried thyme, garlic powder, salt, and pepper.
3. Spread vegetables in a single layer on a baking sheet and roast for 20-25 minutes, flipping halfway through, until tender and golden brown.
4. Meanwhile, season chicken thighs with salt and pepper on both sides.
5. Heat 1 tbsp. olive oil in a large oven-safe skillet over medium-high heat. Add chicken, skin-side down, and cook for 4-5 minutes, until skin is crispy and golden brown.
6. Flip chicken over and transfer skillet to the oven. Bake for 20-25 minutes, until chicken is cooked through and registers an internal temperature of 165°F (74°C).
7. Serve chicken alongside roasted Brussels sprouts and sweet potato wedges.

Quinoa Breakfast Bowl

Ingredients:

- 1/4 cup mixed nuts and seeds (almonds, walnuts, pumpkin seeds)
- 1 tablespoon honey or maple syrup
- 1/2 cup cooked quinoa
- 1/4 cup plain Greek yogurt
- Sliced fruits for topping

Directions:

1. In a bowl, combine cooked quinoa and Greek yogurt.
2. Top with mixed nuts and seeds.
3. Drizzle with honey or maple syrup.
4. Add sliced fruits on top.
5. Stir everything together before eating.

Vegetable Frittata

Ingredients:

- 1/4 cup sliced mushrooms
- 1/4 cup chopped spinach
- Salt and pepper to taste
- 4 large eggs
- a quarter cup of colored bell peppers, chopped
- 1/4 cup chopped onions
- Cooking spray

Directions:

1. Preheat the oven to 350°F (175°C).
2. In a bowl, whisk the eggs with salt and pepper.

3. Heat an oven-safe skillet over medium heat and coat it with cooking spray.
4. Add the bell peppers, onions, and mushrooms to the skillet. Sauté for 2 to 3 minutes or until softened somewhat.
5. Add the spinach and cook for another minute until wilted.
6. 6 . Pour the properly distributed whisked eggs into the skillet.
7. Cook for 2-3 minutes until the edges are set.
8. Transfer the skillet to the preheated oven and bake for 10-12 minutes until the eggs are fully set.
9. Before slicing, take it out of the oven and let it cool for a while.
10. Serve warm.

Oatmeal with Berries and Almonds

Ingredients:

- 1/4 teaspoon vanilla extract
- 1/4 cup mixed berries (blueberries, strawberries, raspberries)
- 1 tablespoon chopped almonds
- 1/2 cup rolled oats
- 1 cup water or low-fat milk
- 1 tablespoon honey or maple syrup

Directions:

1. In a saucepan, combine rolled oats and water or milk.
2. Bring to a boil, then reduce heat to low and simmer for about 5 minutes, stirring occasionally.

3. Stir in the vanilla extract.
4. Transfer the cooked oatmeal to a bowl.
5. Top with mixed berries, chopped almonds, and drizzle with honey or maple syrup.
6. Serve hot.

Roasted Cauliflower And Chickpea Salad With Tahini Dressing

Ingredients:

To prepare Salad:

- 1/2 teaspoon smoked paprika
- Salt and pepper to taste
- 4 cups mixed salad greens
- 1/4 cup chopped fresh cilantro
- 1 head cauliflower, cut into florets
- 1 can chickpeas, drained and rinsed
- Use 2 tablespoon of olive oil
- 1 teaspoon ground cumin

To prepare Tahini Dressing:

- 1/4 cup tahini

- Use 2 tablespoon of fresh lemon juice

- Use 2 tablespoon of water

- 1 clove garlic, minced

- Salt and pepper to taste

Directions:

1. Preheat the oven to 400°F (200°C). On a baking sheet, toss the cauliflower florets and chickpeas with olive oil, ground cumin, smoked paprika, salt, and pepper.
2. Roast for 20-25 minutes or until the cauliflower is golden and tender.
3. In a large bowl, mix the roasted cauliflower and chickpeas with the mixed salad greens and chopped fresh cilantro.
4. In a small bowl, whisk together the tahini, fresh lemon juice, water, minced garlic, salt, and pepper to make the tahini dressing.
5. Drizzle the tahini dressing over the salad and toss gently to ensure all the ingredients are coated.
6. Serve the roasted cauliflower and chickpea salad with tahini dressing immediately.

Watermelon And Feta Salad With Mint And Balsamic Glaze

Ingredients:

- 1/4 cup fresh mint leaves, chopped
- Use 2 tablespoon of balsamic glaze
- 4 cups cubed watermelon
- Use 1 cup of crumbled feta cheese

Directions:

1. In a large bowl, mix the cubed watermelon and crumbled feta cheese.
2. Sprinkle the chopped fresh mint leaves over the watermelon and feta.
3. Drizzle the balsamic glaze over the salad just before serving.

Grilled Portobello Mushroom And Quinoa Salad With Lemon Vinaigrette

Ingredients:

To prepare Salad:

- 4 cups mixed salad greens
- 1/4 cup chopped fresh parsley
- 1/4 cup chopped fresh basil
- 4 large Portobello mushrooms, stems removed
- Use 1 cup of quinoa
- 2 cups water or vegetable broth

To prepare Lemon Vinaigrette:

- Use 2 tablespoon of fresh lemon juice
- 1 teaspoon Dijon mustard

- 1 clove garlic, minced

- 3 tablespoons extra-virgin olive oil

- Salt and pepper to taste

Directions:

1. Preheat the grill or grill pan over medium-high heat. Grill the Portobello mushrooms for 4-5 minutes on each side or until they are tender. Set them aside to cool.
2. Rinse the quinoa under cold water and drain. In a saucepan, bring the water or vegetable broth to a boil.
3. the quinoa, then reduce the heat and simmer for 15-20 minutes or until the quinoa is cooked and the liquid is absorbed. Fluff the quinoa with a fork.
4. In a large bowl, mix the cooked quinoa, mixed salad greens, chopped fresh parsley, and chopped fresh basil.

5. Slice the grilled Portobello mushrooms and add them to the salad.
6. In a small bowl, whisk together the extra-virgin olive oil, fresh lemon juice, Dijon mustard, minced garlic, salt, and pepper to make the lemon vinaigrette.
7. Drizzle the lemon vinaigrette over the salad and toss gently to ensure all ingredients are coated.
8. Serve the grilled Portobello mushroom and quinoa salad with lemon vinaigrette immediately.

Meal-Prep Chili-Lime Chicken Bowls

Ingredients:

- 1 cup julienned jicama
- 1 cup frozen corn, thawed
- 1 cup pico of gallo
- 1 avocado, diced
- ½ cup chopped fresh cilantro
- Lime wedges
- 1 cup cooked quinoa
- 1 cup cooked brown rice
- 1 pound cooked Chili-Lime Chicken (see Associated recipe) (see Associated recipe)
- Hot sauce, such as Cholula

Directions:

1. Combine quinoa and ricedivide into 4 single-serving containers with lids. Top with chicken, jicama, corn, pico de gallo, avocado and cilantro, dividing evenly.
2. Seal the containers and refrigerate for up to 4 days. Serve with lime wedges and spicy sauce.

Chopped Cobb Salad

Ingredients:

- 1 pound of ground beef

- 1 diced hard-boiled egg.

- 1 tbsp. blue cheese crumbles

- 3 cups of iceberg lettuce finely chopped

- Chopped chicken thigh from a baked chicken (see associated recipe)

- 1 chopped celery stalk

- Vinaigrette made with 2 tablespoons honey-mustard (see associated recipe)

Directions:

1. In order to begin, you must first complete Step 1.

2. Chop the ingredients for the salad and place them in a bowl or a container that can be sealed.
3. Pour the dressing on top of the salad just before serving.

Banana Nut Pancakes

Ingredients:

- 1/4 teaspoon salt

- 1 cup mashed ripe bananas (about 2 medium bananas)

- 3/4 cup buttermilk

- 1 large egg

- 2 tablespoons unsalted butter, melted

- 1/2 teaspoon vanilla extract

- 1 cup all-purpose flour

- 2 tablespoons sugar

- 1 teaspoon baking powder

- 1/2 teaspoon baking soda

- 1/3 cup chopped nuts (walnuts or pecans)

Directions:

1. In a large mixing bowl, whisk together the flour, sugar, baking powder, baking soda, and salt.
2. In a separate bowl, combine the mashed bananas, buttermilk, egg, melted butter, and vanilla extract. Mix until well combined.
3. Pour the wet ingredients into the dry ingredients. Stir until just combined. Be careful not to over mixsome lumps are okay. Fold in the chopped nuts.
4. Heat a griddle or non-stick skillet over medium heat. Lightly grease with cooking spray or butter.
5. Pour 1/4 cup portions of batter onto the griddle for each pancake. Cook until bubbles form on the surface, then flip and cook the other side until golden brown.

6. Stack the pancakes on a plate and serve with your favorite toppings, such as sliced bananas, maple syrup, or additional nuts.

Smoothie Bowl

Ingredients:

For the Smoothie Base:

- 1/2 cup plain Greek yogurt

- 1/2 cup almond milk (or any milk of your choice)

- 1 tablespoon chia seeds (optional)

- 1 frozen banana

- 1/2 cup frozen mixed berries (such as strawberries, blueberries, and raspberries)

- 1/2 cup spinach leaves (fresh or frozen)

Toppings:

- Sliced fresh fruits (e.g., banana, kiwi, berries)

- Granola

- Nuts and seeds (e.g., almonds, chia seeds)
- Shredded coconut
- Drizzle of honey or maple syrup (optional)

Directions:

1. In a blender, combine the frozen banana, mixed berries, spinach, Greek yogurt, almond milk, and chia seeds.
2. Blend until smooth and creamy. Adjust the consistency by adding more milk if needed.
3. Slice fresh fruits and set aside.
4. Measure out granola, nuts, seeds, and shredded coconut.
5. Pour the smoothie base into a bowl.
6. Arrange the sliced fruits, granola, nuts, seeds, and shredded coconut on top of the smoothie.
7. Add a touch of sweetness if desired.

Egg And Spinach Breakfast Wrap

Ingredients:

- 1/4 cup cherry tomatoes, diced
- 1/4 cup feta cheese, crumbled
- Salt and pepper to taste
- 2 large eggs
- 1 cup fresh spinach, chopped
- 1 whole-wheat or multigrain wrap
- Olive oil (for cooking)

Directions:

1. Heat a small amount of olive oil in a pan over medium heat.
2. Add chopped spinach and sauté until wilted. Season with salt and pepper. Set aside.

3. In the same pan, crack the eggs and scramble them. Cook until just set.
4. Lay the whole-wheat wrap on a flat surface.
5. Spread the scrambled eggs in the center of the wrap.
6. Add the sautéed spinach on top of the eggs.
7. Sprinkle diced cherry tomatoes and crumbled feta cheese over the eggs and spinach.
8. Fold the sides of the wrap over the filling, creating a wrap shape.
9. Place the wrap back in the pan for a minute to warm it up and melt the cheese slightly.
10. Remove from the pan and serve immediately.

Mediterranean Breakfast Bowls

Ingredients:

- 1 cup or 140gm cherry tomatoes

- Extra virgin olive oil, as needed

- 1 cup or 30gm arugula or butter head lettuce

- 5 to 6 or 36gm calamite olives, pitted

- 2 eggs or 80gm

- 3/4 cup or 188gm hummus, homemade or store-bought

- 4 oz. Or 113gm white mushrooms, halved

- 1 or 3gm garlic clove, finely minced

- ½ of 1 scallion or 5gm

Directions:

1. First, cook the eggs as per your desire. You can go for scrambled eggs or sunny-side-up, or soft-boiled eggs.
2. After that, heat a large skillet over medium heat, and spoon in the oil. Once heated, stir in the mushrooms and cook for 6 to 7 minutes or until the mushrooms are browned on both sides.
3. Then, add the cherry tomatoes, garlic, and spinach to it. Sauté them for 2 to 3 minutes or until the spinach is wilted.
4. Finally, assemble the bowls by dividing the mushroom mixture among the two bowls and then add the eggs and hummus. Spoon in a bit of olive oil over it.
5. Taste for seasoning and add more if needed. Tip: Seasonings like zaatar would be a good choice.
6. Serve hot and enjoy.

Mango Ginger Smoothie Bowl

Ingredients:

- Dash of Cinnamon, ground

- 1 tsp. or 7gm Honey, or optional

- 1 tsp. or 2gm Ginger, fresh & chopped

- ¼ cup or 62gm Greek Yogurt, vanilla & low-fat or Soy Yogurt

- ½ cup banana or 150gm, mashed

- 1 cup or 165gm Mango chunks, frozen

- ½ cup or 100gm Chickpeas, cooked

- 3 Ice Cubes

- ¼ cup or 32ml Carrot Juice

- 1 tsp. Hemp Hearts

Directions:

1. Start by placing chickpeas, mango, carrot juice, ginger, honey, and cardamom in a high-speed lender.
2. Blend them for 2 to 3 minutes or until they become smooth, thick, and creamy. Tip: If it seems too thick, add one to two take spoons of dairy or non-dairy milk.
3. Finally, transfer them to the bowl and enjoy. Top it with the hemp heart.

Raspberry Overnight Muesli

Ingredients:

- ½ cup or 45gm Old-fashioned Rolled Oats
- ½ cup Raspberries or 60gm, preferably frozen
- ¾ cup or 184gm Yogurt, non-fat & vanilla
- 1 tablespoon or 8.12gm Almonds, chopped
- 2 tablespoons or 20gm Chia Seeds

Directions:

1. First, place yogurt and oats in a medium-sized owl and then mix until combined.
2. Next, cover the bowl with a plastic wring and keep it in the refrigerator overnight.
3. Before serving, top it with the almonds and raspberries.
4. Serve and enjoy.

Grilled Eggplant With Tomato Sauce And Oregano

Ingredients:

- 2 ripe tomatoes
- 2 tablespoons of tomato paste
- 1 clove of garlic, finely chopped
- 1 teaspoon dried oregano (or a few fresh oregano leaves)
- eggplants
- Extra virgin olive oil
- Salt and pepper.

Directions:

1. Preheat the grill over medium-high heat.

2. Cut the aubergines into slices about 1 cm thick. Brush both sides of the eggplant slices with olive oil and season with salt and pepper.
3. Grill the eggplant slices for about 3 to 4 minutes per side, until soft and have nice streaks from the grill. Remove the eggplants from the grill and set them aside.
4. Meanwhile, prepare the tomato sauce. Chop the ripe tomatoes or puree them to obtain a smooth texture. In a pan, heat a drizzle of olive oil and add the minced garlic. Cook the garlic for a few minutes until it turns golden.
5. Add the chopped or pureed tomatoes to the pan along with the tomato paste. Season with dried oregano, salt and pepper. Cook over medium-low heat for about 10 to 15 minutes, stirring occasionally, until the sauce thickens and the flavors develop.
6. Once ready, place the grilled aubergine slices on a serving plate.

7. Pour the hot tomato sauce over the grilled eggplants.
8. You can decorate with a few fresh oregano leaves.
9. Serve the grilled eggplants with tomato sauce and oregano as a tasty appetizer or side dish.
10. You can customize this recipe by adding grated cheese on top of the aborigines and gratin them in the oven for a few minutes, or by adding crushed red pepper flakes for a touch of spiciness.
11. These grilled eggplants with tomato and oregano salsa are a delicious option for a vegetarian meal or as a side dish for a summer lunch or dinner.

Black Olive Paté With Croutons Of Whole Meal Bread

Ingredients:

- Juice of 1/2 lemon
- 2 tablespoons of extra virgin olive oil
- Ground black pepper
- 200 g of pitted black olives
- 2 anchovy fillets in oil
- 1 clove of garlic
- Croutons of whole meal bread to serve.

Directions:

1. Start by rinsing the black olives under running water to remove excess salt.

2. Put the pitted black olives, the anchovy fillets in oil, the minced garlic clove, the lemon juice and the extra virgin olive oil in a mixer or food processor.
3. Blend the ingredients until you get a smooth and homogeneous consistency.
4. Taste the black olive paté and adjust the flavor by adding ground black pepper according to your personal taste.
5. Transfer the black olive pâté to a serving bowl.
6. Serve the black olive paté with croutons of whole meal bread as a tasty appetizer.
7. To make whole meal croutons, cut slices of whole meal bread and toast them in the oven or on the grill until crispy. You can brush the slices of bread with a little olive oil and rub them with a clove of garlic for extra flavor.
8. The black olive pâté is full of flavor and goes perfectly with croutons of whole meal bread.

9. You can also add a few fresh basil leaves or a drizzle of extra virgin olive oil on top of the pate to decorate.
10. This appetizer is ideal for a special occasion or for an aperitif with friends.

Smoked Salmon Mousse With Whole Meal Crackers

Ingredients:

- Juice of 1/2 lemon
- 2 tablespoons of mayonnaise
- 1 tablespoon fresh chives, finely chopped
- Salt and pepper
- 200 g of smoked salmon
- 200 g of cream cheese (such as Philadelphia)
- Wholegrain crackers to serve.

Directions:

1. Start by cutting the smoked salmon into smaller pieces to make it easier to work with.

2. Place the smoked salmon, cream cheese, lemon juice, mayonnaise and chives in a mixer or food processor.
3. Blend the ingredients until you get a smooth and creamy consistency.
4. Taste the smoked salmon mousse and adjust the seasoning to your personal taste, adding salt and pepper if needed.
5. Transfer the smoked salmon mousse to a serving bowl.
6. Serve smoked salmon mousse with whole grain crackers as a delicious appetizer.
7. You can customize this recipe by adding ingredients like extra lemon juice for a fresher flavor or a sprinkle of pink peppercorn on top of the mousse for a more eye-catching presentation.
8. Wholegrain crackers are perfect to accompany smoked salmon mousse, but you

can also opt for slices of toasted bread or bread sticks.
9. This appetizer is ideal for an elegant dinner or a special occasion.

Pineapple Coconut Smoothie

Ingredients:

- 1/2 cup Greek yogurt
- 1 tablespoon honey or maple syrup (optional, for added sweetness)
- 1/4 teaspoon vanilla extract
- 1 cup frozen pineapple chunks
- 1/2 cup coconut milk (unsweetened)
- 1/4 cup shredded coconut (optional, for garnish)

Directions:

1. In a blender, mix together the frozen pineapple chunks, coconut milk, Greek yogurt, honey or maple syrup (if desired), and vanilla extract.

2. Blend the ingredients on high speed until the mixture is smooth and creamy, making sure there are no large chunks of pineapple left.
3. Once the smoothie is ready, pour it into glasses. Optional: Top each glass with a sprinkle of shredded coconut for extra flavor and texture.

Oat Bran With Berries

Ingredients:

- 1 tablespoon honey or maple syrup (optional)
- 1 tablespoon chopped nuts (almonds, walnuts, or pecans) for garnish (optional)
- A pinch of cinnamon (optional)
- 1/2 cup oat bran
- 1 cup water or milk (dairy or plant-based)
- 1/2 cup mixed berries (strawberries, blueberries, raspberries)

Directions:

1. In a saucepan, heat the water or milk over medium heat until it boils.
2. Once boiling, add the oat bran and reduce the heat to a simmer.

3. Cook the oat bran for 3-5 minutes, stirring occasionally, until it reaches the desired thickness.
4. When it's done, transfer the oat bran to a bowl.
5. To finish, top the oat bran with mixed berries, drizzle with honey or maple syrup (optional), and sprinkle chopped nuts or a pinch of cinnamon for extra flavor.

Quinoa Breakfast Porridge

Ingredients:

- 1 tablespoon honey or maple syrup (optional)
- 1/4 teaspoon ground cinnamon
- 1 tablespoon chopped nuts (almonds, walnuts, or pecans) for garnish (optional)
- A dash of vanilla extract (optional)
- 1/2 cup quinoa (rinsed)
- 1 cup water or milk (dairy or plant-based)
- 1/2 cup diced apples or mixed berries

Directions:

1. In a saucepan, combine the rinsed quinoa and either water or milk.

2. Bring it to a boil over medium-high heat, then reduce the heat to low, cover the saucepan, and let it simmer for 15-20 minutes or until the quinoa is cooked and the liquid is absorbed. Stir occasionally.
3. Once the quinoa is cooked, add the diced apples or mixed berries, honey or maple syrup (if desired), ground cinnamon, and a dash of vanilla extract (if desired).
4. Cook for an additional 2-3 minutes until the fruits are softened and the flavors are blended.
5. Serve the quinoa porridge in bowls and top with chopped nuts for a crunchy texture.

Whole Grain Pasta Dishes With Tomatoes Sauce

Ingredients:

- 1/4 cup chopped fresh basil
- 2 cloves garlic, minced
- 12 oz whole wheat spaghetti
- 2 cups diced tomatoes
- 1 tbsp olive oil

Directions:

1. Cook spaghetti according to package instructions.
2. Warm the olive oil in a large pan over medium heat and Cook for 1-2 minutes after adding garlic.
1. Add diced tomatoes to the skillet and simmer for 5 minutes.
3. Add chopped basil to the skillet and stir well.

4. Add the spaghetti to the skillet after draining it. Mix well to evenly coat the spaghetti with the sauce.
5. Serve hot.

Whole Grain Penne With Roasted Tomatoes And Garlic Sauce

Ingredients:

- 3 cloves garlic, minced
- 2 tbsp olive oil
- 1 tsp dried oregano
- 12 oz whole grain penne pasta
- 2 cups cherry tomatoes
- Salt and pepper to taste

Directions:

1. Preheat the oven to 400°F.
2. In a baking dish, toss the cherry tomatoes, minced garlic, olive oil, dried oregano, salt, and pepper.

3. Roast in the oven for 15-20 minutes, or until the tomatoes are soft and slightly charred.
4. Cook penne pasta according to package instructions.
5. Drain the cooked pasta and add it to the roasted tomatoes and garlic sauce. Mix well to combine.
6. Serve hot.

Whole Wheat Fairdale With Tomato, Spinach, And Mushroom Sauce

Ingredients:

- 1 cup sliced mushrooms
- 1/4 cup diced onion
- 2 cloves garlic, minced
- 12 oz whole wheat farfalle pasta
- 2 cups diced tomatoes
- 2 cups fresh spinach
- 1 tbsp olive oil

Directions:

1. Cook the farfalle pasta according to package instructions.

2. In a large skillet, heat olive oil over medium heat. Cook for 1-2 minutes after adding onions and garlic.
3. Add diced tomatoes to the skillet and cook for 5 minutes.
4. Add sliced mushrooms to the skillet and cook for an additional 5 minutes.
5. Stir in fresh spinach and cook until wilted.
6. Drain the cooked pasta and add it to the skillet with the tomato, spinach, and mushroom sauce. Mix well to coat the pasta.
7. Serve hot.

Tomato Basil Quiche

Ingredients:

- Whole wheat pie crust

- Eggs

- Cherry tomatoes, halved

- Fresh basil, chopped

- Low-fat milk

Directions:

1. Preheat oven to 375°F (190°C).
2. Whisk eggs and milk, then pour into pie crust.
3. Add tomatoes and basil on top.
4. Bake until the quiche is set and golden.

Grilled Lemon Herb Salmon

Ingredients:

- 1 teaspoon dried herbs (rosemary, thyme, oregano)
- Juice of 1 lemon
- 1 salmon fillet
- 1 tablespoon olive oil

Directions:

1. Preheat grill to medium-high heat.
2. Brush salmon with olive oil, sprinkle with herbs, and squeeze lemon juice over it.
3. Grill for 6-8 minutes per side or until the salmon flakes easily.

Grilled Vegetable Wrap With Hummus And Baby Carrots.

Ingredients:

- 4 whole wheat tortillas
- 1/2 cup hummus
- 1/2 cup baby carrots
- 2 tablespoons olive oil
- 1 medium zucchini, sliced lengthwise
- 1 medium red bell pepper, sliced into strips
- 1 medium yellow onion, sliced into rings
- Salt and pepper to taste

Directions:

1. Preheat a grill or grill pan over medium-high heat.

2. Brush the zucchini, red bell pepper, and onion with olive oil and sprinkle with salt and pepper.
3. Grill the vegetables until they are tender and slightly charred, about 5-7 minutes per side.
4. Warm the tortillas in the microwave or on the grill for 10-20 seconds.
5. Spread 2 tablespoons of hummus on each tortilla.
6. Divide the grilled vegetables evenly between the tortillas.
7. Roll up the tortillas, tucking in the ends, to make wraps.
8. Serve with baby carrots on the side.

Black Bean And Vegetable Chili With A Side Of Whole-Grain Cornbread.

Ingredients:

- 1/4 teaspoon cayenne pepper
- 1 can black beans, drained and rinsed
- 1 can diced tomatoes, undrained
- 1 cup vegetable broth
- 1/2 teaspoon salt
- 1/4 teaspoon black pepper
- 2 tablespoons chopped fresh cilantro
- 1 tablespoon lime juice
- 1 tablespoon olive oil
- 1 onion, chopped

- 3 cloves garlic, minced

- 1 red bell pepper, chopped

- 1 zucchini, chopped

- 1 tablespoon chili powder

- 1 teaspoon ground cumin

- 1/2 teaspoon smoked paprika

For the whole-grain cornbread:

- 1 cup whole wheat flour

- 1 cup cornmeal

- 1 tablespoon baking powder

- 1/2 teaspoon salt

- 1/4 cup honey or maple syrup

- 1 cup milk (dairy or non-dairy)

- 2 eggs

- 1/4 cup melted butter or oil

Directions:

1. Heat the olive oil in a large pot over medium heat. Add the onion and garlic and cook until the onion is soft and translucent, about 5 minutes.
2. Add the red bell pepper and zucchini and cook until they start to soften, about 5 more minutes.
3. Add the chili powder, cumin, smoked paprika, and cayenne pepper and stir to combine.
4. Add the black beans, diced tomatoes, vegetable broth, salt, and black pepper. Bring the mixture to a simmer and cook for about 15 minutes.
5. While the chili is cooking, preheat the oven to 400°F (200°C). Grease an 8-inch square baking dish.

6. In a medium bowl, whisk together the whole wheat flour, cornmeal, baking powder, and salt.
7. In another bowl, whisk together the honey or maple syrup, milk, eggs, and melted butter or oil.
8. Add the wet ingredients to the dry ingredients and stir until just combined. Pour the batter into the prepared baking dish.
9. Bake the cornbread for about 20-25 minutes, or until a toothpick inserted into the center comes out clean.
10. When the chili is done, stir in the cilantro and lime juice. Serve hot with a slice of cornbread on the side.

Greek Yogurt With Sliced Peaches And Chopped Almonds.

Ingredients:

- 1 cup Greek yogurt
- 1 peach, sliced
- 1/4 cup chopped almonds

Directions:

1. Place the Greek yogurt in a bowl.
2. Add the sliced peaches on top.
3. Sprinkle the chopped almonds over the peaches and yogurt.
4. Serve and enjoy!

www.ingramcontent.com/pod-product-compliance
Lightning Source LLC
LaVergne TN
LVHW010219070526
838199LV00062B/4663